WEDDING TOASTS 101

The Guide to the Perfect Wedding Speech

PETE HONSBERGER

Adams Media

New York London Toronto Sydney New Delhi

A **adams**media

Adams Media
An Imprint of Simon & Schuster, Inc.
57 Littlefield Street
Avon, Massachusetts 02322

First Adams Media hardcover edition November 2019

ADAMS MEDIA and colophon are trademarks of Simon & Schuster.

For information about special discounts for bulk purchases, please contact Simon & Schuster Special Sales at 1-866-506-1949 or business@simonandschuster.com.

The Simon & Schuster Speakers Bureau can bring authors to your live event. For more information or to book an event contact the Simon & Schuster Speakers Bureau at 1-866-248-3049 or visit our website at www.simonspeakers.com.

Interior design by Priscilla Yuen
Interior images by Priscilla Yuen; © 123RF/ Ekaterina Kondrateva, Anna Konstantinova, Tatiana Kostysheva, lineartestpilot, Elena Matveeva, mevar, Chanin Nuisin, Aliaksandr Siamko, Diana Johanna Velasquez

Manufactured in the United States of America

10 9 8 7 6 5 4 3 2

Library of Congress Cataloging-in-Publication Data
Names: Honsberger, Pete, author.
Title: Wedding toasts 101 / Pete Honsberger.
Description: Avon, Massachusetts: Adams Media, 2019.
Includes index.
Identifiers: LCCN 2019023096 | ISBN 9781507210765 (hc) | ISBN 9781507210772 (ebook)
Subjects: LCSH: Wedding toasts.
Classification: LCC PN6348.W4 H66 2019 | DDC 809.5/12--dc23
LC record available at https://lccn.loc.gov/2019023096

ISBN 978-1-5072-1076-5
ISBN 978-1-5072-1077-2 (ebook)

DEDICATION

This book is dedicated to you, who won't take
this honor and responsibility lightly.
Have some fun with it too.

ACKNOWLEDGMENTS

For anyone who has helped make this project possible, I cannot thank you enough. To Jenna, the love of my life: thank you for your constant support and encouragement, and the kicks in the butt to keep going. To my parents, Jim and Kathy, for the help and kind words along the way. To my brothers and sister-in-law: thanks for being there as I brainstormed ideas. Special thanks to Dan and Kate Honsberger for giving me my first wedding toast opportunity and providing huge inspiration for this book.

To Brian and Carli Velbeck for the ideas and permission to refer to your wedding, which was amazing. To Rich and Katie Velbeck, who put up with a loud interruption in their best men toast. To Matt Huml, who tossed me some incredibly helpful feedback: I'm counting on you to buy copies of this if no one else will.

To John Lee Dumas and Kate Erickson for *The Freedom Journal*, which was a catalyst for this project. To the TFJ Community: I am honored to have completed a goal alongside you.

A sincere thank-you to anyone who read and shot holes in my first draft, including Lindsay Foster, Leigh McDermott, Jenna, Mom, Dan, and Kate.

Lastly, thanks to you for reading. This investment will pay huge dividends in your toast. And if it doesn't, I'll buy you a drink.

CONTENTS

INTRODUCTION

The first look, the vows, the dances...the toasts. If you are reading this, there's a good chance you've been personally selected by a friend, family member, or even third cousin twice removed to speak at this important event in their life. Maybe you're the best man. Maybe you're the maid of honor. Or maybe you're a longtime family friend. But no matter who you are, your name will be eternally embossed on the wedding ceremony program, and what you say (and how you say it) matters.

Starting to feel a bit nervous? Take a deep breath and fear not; you've come to the right place! *Wedding Toasts 101* is your all-inclusive guide to creating and executing an unforgettable wedding toast. You'll discover everything you need, including:

- Questions to ask yourself as you write your toast
- Prompts to get your creative juices flowing
- Tips on dealing with reception annoyances, like bad lighting and echoing acoustics
- Case studies on specific toast challenges and themes
- The five critical "cogs" of a great toast
- Main takeaways at the end of each chapter
- A complete wedding toast checklist

You'll also find an appendix with examples of great toasts, so you can see how real wedding guests have honored, amused, and affected family members, friends, and strangers alike.

Your speech, your audience, and especially the happy couple deserve the very best that you have to offer, and with the tools and practical advice in this book, you'll be sure to deliver on that promise. So are you ready to get started? You've got a wedding toast to give!

Part 1

SO YOU'VE BEEN ASKED TO TOAST

"**W**e're engaged!" You receive the news over lunch, during drinks, or maybe via a surprise phone call, and suddenly a loved one is taking a big step in their life—and they want you to toast the occasion. This is great news! So how do you feel? You're probably excited and honored to share in their special day, but soon a sense of responsibility comes over you. In a few short months, you (who may not particularly enjoy speaking in front of, well, anyone) will be standing in front of a crowd of wedding guests, with all eyes fixed on you. You find yourself wondering, *How can I truly honor this person? How do I give an unforgettable toast?*

In this part of the book, you'll discover the answers to these questions and more. You'll learn why great toasts can feel difficult to write, and what challenges you may face when the time comes to deliver your speech. You'll hear stories of challenges real people have dealt with, and also discover the key "dos and don'ts" of a great toast. Here, the groundwork for your toast is laid out—you just need to turn the page.

CHAPTER 1

Toasting Ain't Easy: Main Challenges

Regardless of who you are, and your level of writing skill or speaking competency, delivering a wedding toast can be pretty intimidating. Aside from the actual moment you stand up to speak (you didn't notice how many people were there until now, did you?!), there's the content of your toast, all of the different personal stories and ideas you want to squeeze into it, and the simple fact that you get only one shot at this honor. A major part of your success is knowing what is toast-worthy and what isn't: Would the groom want you to share that embarrassing (though admittedly funny) anecdote from a college party? Would a crowd of people be interested in the lengthy background story of your working relationship with the bride?

This chapter lays out the different kinds of stories you *should* share with your audience, as well as the ones you should keep to yourself. You'll also explore other challenges you may not have considered before, such as reception hall acoustics and audience restlessness. You'll be able to turn past experiences with the toastee(s) into a compelling narrative that'll have everyone talking—even after the special day. After all, when the cake has been eaten, the DJ has packed up their gear, and the guests have started shuffling out, these are the memories that will remain.

IT'S PERSONAL

A big part of why the wedding toast can seem so daunting is because it is personal. You will be standing up to express how you feel about the couple in front of you, and sharing in a truly special event in their lives. And what could be more personal than a moment shared with people you love? It's why you see tears during the bridal procession and misty eyes throughout the first dance. It's why friends and family members throw engagement parties and bridal showers, travel great distances, and do whatever it takes to be a part of this momentous event.

Whether you are a family member or friend (or both!), this person has chosen you specifically to speak on their special day. Because of the nature of your relationship with one or both members of the happy couple, you have a unique perspective—and great stories to tell. Who else knows the details of the seventh-grade dance that produced photos of objectively *terrible* fashion choices? Who can recount better than you the day the bride or groom told you about meeting the future love of their life?

🔍 CASE STUDY **Childhood Mischief**

In the rhyming toast I gave at my brother Dan's wedding, I included the following:

Dan's been an outstanding big brother; I couldn't ask for any more.
Though he did once try to build a campfire in his bedroom and
burned a hole in the floor…

This brief tidbit came from an experience in our childhood, when Dan thought it would be a good idea to use baseball cards to start a miniature campfire in his bedroom. This story illustrated Dan's curiosity and love for the outdoors (and bringing it *indoors*), worked into a fun rhyme that kept the audience engaged. His wedding was the first time that many of his wife's family members met him, and while very brief, this story humanized Dan and provided a way for them to relate to him. After all, just about everyone has silly stories about the trouble they got into as a kid. The audience was able to identify with him and also share a laugh over it. It even became a fun topic of discussion the next day at brunch.

Can you tell an audience, some of whom are probably half in the bag already, everything about that person in a ten-minute speech? Of course not. Can you share a few compelling tidbits about your relationship that showcase their character? Absolutely, and you should! While you can't make the speech in the special language the two of you created as kids, you can share unique experiences from your relationship that connect the audience to that person—and perhaps also their partner—even more.

WEDDING TOAST WORKOUT:
Yay or Nay

So how can you know for certain whether a story is appropriate to share during your toast? The following is a three-part litmus test to get a definitive "yay" or "nay" on a story you are thinking about using:

1. **Interest:** Tell your story aloud to yourself. If you laugh, smile, or get a little teary, the story has passed step 1. If not, scrap it.

2. **Context:** Now, close your eyes and envision yourself going to a wedding as a date. You may have met the bride and groom, but calling them "acquaintances" would still be a stretch. Picture this exact story being told at the wedding by someone else. If it makes you emotional, piques your interest, or makes you smile or laugh, the story has passed step 2. If not, keep it in your own memory.

3. **Obsession:** Simply put, are you obsessed with this story and dying to share it at the wedding? Would the toast feel incomplete without it? If you feel strongly that it needs to be included, the story has passed step 3. If not, let it go.

The key takeaway to remember here is that you want your toast to resonate with even the casual listener. You can include one or two inside jokes, as this will add to the intrigue, but avoid more than that. You're part archaeologist and part translator for the audience. To do this right, you'll be digging up golden artifacts about the bride or groom and delivering them in a way that the wedding guests will understand.

OTHER HURDLES

Beyond balancing personal stories with connecting to the rest of the audience, there are a few obstacles you may face when it comes time to actually deliver your toast. For example, is there anything more irritating than a squeaky microphone when you are trying to describe a fond memory about the bride? Unfortunately, things can happen when you take center stage. What are they exactly, and how might you nip them in the bud? The following are the key difficulties you may encounter as you raise your glass to the happy couple. Considering these *before* the special day can help ensure that everything goes according to plan.

Audio Issues

Not being heard clearly by the audience is one of the biggest obstacles when giving a toast. Microphones aren't always clear and can sometimes give annoying feedback; acoustics in the room may not be ideal; and it's easy to fall into a trap of either swallowing the mic or holding it too far away for anyone sitting past the first table to hear you. If you're able to practice at the venue beforehand, do so. You can also ask around to see if anyone you know has been to that venue before and has insight into the room's acoustics.

If the room is small, you can get away with having the microphone farther away from your mouth, and you can speak a bit faster (if necessary). In bigger rooms, however, it is critical to talk slower and keep the microphone close to your mouth. An easy tip for mastering the mic is to ask a friend in advance to give you a nod (yes) or a headshake (no) after you say the first line of your toast to show whether you are being heard clearly.

CASE STUDY **An Acoustic-y Situation**

Anytime the wedding venue is a giant lobby or room with really high ceilings and a lot of open space, the sound acoustics are likely to present some challenges. One wedding in particular took place in a grand old lobby where sound was constantly bouncing off every wall and the ceiling. Anticipating these sound issues ahead of time, the maid of honor and best man both acknowledged to the crowd right away that they'd make an extra effort to speak clearly, and slowed down the speed of their toasts a bit so the audience could better pick up on every word despite the echoing room. It can be so tempting to fly through your toast, but especially in a situation like this, your words would sound like the blurred horn of a train. Instead, the maid of honor and best man were able to adapt to the bad acoustics and be understood by their audience.

Lighting

Will you be in an area where people can see your face clearly? Will there be a spotlight on you that may be blindingly bright or warm to the point of sweating? Maybe you can't know the answer for sure until you get up to give your toast, but there *are* a few ways to improve a bad lighting situation.

First, find the head table and note how lit up it is compared to the rest of the room; chances are, your toast will take place very close to that table. Also, remember that when you are handed a microphone, the room belongs to you. Don't be afraid to walk into a better lighting situation while you're delivering your opening lines, as long as the microphone wire permits it. There's no wedding rule that says you have to stand in one place during a speech. Always assume that someone is filming your toast and that the happy couple will want to watch it again later, so make it as easy as possible for everyone to both hear and see you.

Audience Restlessness

If there are any young kids, or friends or relatives who can get a bit rowdy, on the guest list, it may be harder to grab everyone's attention and keep the room quiet. With a great toast, this won't be as much of a problem for you; however, if you find yourself needing to get better control of the crowd, there are a few things you can do. First, once you accept the microphone, hold it for a few seconds without saying a word. Or, simply say, "Good evening" and then take a long pause. This silence will get the audience's attention, and anyone talking will realize that you're not going to continue until they quiet down. If you're not comfortable with a long pause, here are a few phrases you can use to politely (and humorously) ask for the audience's attention:

- "I realize I'm standing between you and the reopening of the bar, so I'll get right to it."
- "As soon as we're all settled in, I'll share [bride or groom's] deepest, darkest secret."
- "Can I get a quick round of applause for the bride and the groom before I start?"
- "As soon as I have your attention, the roast will begin." [wink]

Following Another Great Speech

It can be intimidating to speak after someone else, especially when their toast was such a success. While the tools in this book will help you capture your audience's attention, there are a few things you can also do in the moment should you find yourself feeling more nervous when following a great toast. First, acknowledge the previous speaker. Give them kudos for doing an amazing job, and perhaps make a quip about feeling as though you are following Tiger Woods onto the eighteenth green or Gisele Bündchen down the runway. You'll pay homage to the previous speaker's skill and at the same time transition the audience favorably to what you have to say. Remember that the purpose of the toasts is to honor and entertain the newly wedded couple; you *want* the person toasting before you to do a great job. And now it's your opportunity to keep the standard high.

🔍 CASE STUDY **Room Logistics**

When a friend of mine got married a few years ago, I was invited to drop in as a surprise speaker during the toast given by the two best men. The challenges I had during this impromptu speech were where to stand while the best men were speaking, how to keep it a surprise from the bride and groom until it was my time to speak, and how to begin speaking when it was my turn. The room was long and narrow, and our table happened to be tucked away toward the back of the room, which actually helped with my element of surprise! When the toast began, I moved closer to the main table, leaning myself against a nearby wall without garnering much attention. After all, all eyes were on the current speakers. To further reduce any suspicion, I pulled out my phone and took a few pictures of the best men. To anyone else in the room, I was just standing there for a better picture of the action. Then, when I got the signal from the best men, I said my opening line and strolled out to the middle of the floor while a gasping audience waited to see whether this was planned or I had just crashed the toast. The surprise was a hit, and my additional words made the best men's toast just a bit more special for the bride and groom.

CHAPTER SUMMARY

Here, you will find a quick recap of the important information in this chapter. If there is anything you take away from the previous sections, it should be the following:

- Remember that you were chosen for a reason. You have special insights to offer about the person/happy couple, so share them!
- Consider whether a story is crucial to your toast or if it is better kept to yourself. No, the bride's grandmother does *not* need to know about the bride's wine-chugging skills.
- Plan ahead! While you can't predict the future, you can anticipate things that might affect your toast (pesky microphone feedback included), so consider all of these factors beforehand.

CHAPTER 2

Toast "Don'ts"

You've aimed the spotlight on those often overlooked challenges when giving a wedding toast—and now it's time to turn that discerning eye toward yourself. While you maintain creative control over your toast, there are some key "don'ts" you should keep in mind as you write and deliver your speech. These things may seem like good ideas as you are writing—heck, they may have been hilarious in that online wedding video or favorite rom-com—but ultimately, they will have your audience rolling their eyes, losing interest, or even eyeing the exit doors.

In this chapter, you'll take a look at the most common ways people turn a great wedding toast into an event that the newlyweds and their guests would rather forget. From offensive comments about the mother of the bride to one too many pre-toast drinks, you'll be fully briefed on these major "don'ts" so you can focus your energy on the "dos." You'll be able to dodge the most common mistakes and give a toast worth remembering. You are working hard on this special moment, and the proactive measures in this chapter will keep you on track for the best toast possible.

WHAT NOT TO DO

The truth is that things happen. Whether someone isn't prepared, goes into panic mode, or misjudges their audience, people can and do make mistakes when giving a speech. Luckily, knowing the most common mistakes and how to overcome them will be the difference between applause and uncomfortable silence when it is your turn to take the microphone. To ensure that your toast has a positive and memorable impact on your audience, avoid the following pitfalls.

Don't Lose Your Nerve

This includes things like nervous laughter, reading straight from your phone or a piece of paper, and stumbling over your words. Of course, that doesn't mean that it's wrong or unnatural to feel nervous about giving your toast, or to refer to your phone or a piece of paper once in a while as you speak. And no matter how many times you practice ahead of time, you may still stumble over a sentence or make a nervous gesture. That's okay! After all, nothing is perfect—and neither is any person. This "don't" is about a lack of preparation that has you feeling overwhelmed and that ultimately takes over the whole moment, making the audience uncomfortable in the process.

If you do read from a piece of paper, don't write too small or sloppily, with scratched out words and arrows rearranging the order of things. Take an extra few minutes to rewrite a clean copy before

you get up in front of the crowd. You may want to include bullet points to expand on rather than full blocks of text to skim over as you speak. If that's the case, rehearse each point out loud beforehand. Don't fumble because you wrote something too simple, like "Summer Trip 2014," skipped rehearsing, and now can't recall what you meant to say about the trip. If you'll be reading from a cell phone instead, make sure it has plenty of juice. Additionally, change your screen settings to keep it unlocked. You don't want your cell phone to lock while you're expanding on a point, forcing your audience to wait in silence as you type in your passcode and try to recover your place in the toast.

CASE STUDY **The iPad Lesson**

I was once in the audience at a wedding reception where a toast was being read directly from an app on an iPad. Since tablets have bigger screens than cell phones, the thought behind this made sense—the execution, though, was a different story. A few minutes in, the toast giver accidentally closed the app. She apologized while scrambling to reopen it, and tried to fill the silence in these long thirty seconds, providing obvious filler information (that she was trying to reopen the app, etc.) unrelated to the bride or groom. A few minutes later, after restarting the app and continuing her toast, the iPad screen became locked and she had to stop again, this time to unlock the tablet and regain her place. These distractions took away from the impact of the toast and made it feel rocky and ill-prepared.

Don't Make Cringe-Worthy Comments

If you're planning to add in some humor or a few soft jabs at the bride and the groom, remember that while light roasting of a loved one can be funny, there is a line to be drawn. What you might find funny while jotting down notes for your toast may very well come across as uncomfortable or inappropriate to the newlyweds and their other guests. So, what qualifies as cringe-worthy? Here are a few common examples:

- **References to specific exes.** No one wants to hear a comparison of the bride to the groom's ex-girlfriend from college. The groom doesn't want to think about the bride's first relationship in high school as he's raising a glass to the next chapter of his life with her. A very general "When I met John, I could tell he was different from any of Amy's previous boyfriends" is fine, but this toast is not about past relationships; it is about the married couple and their future together.

- **Any story where the focal point is drinking or doing drugs.** By all means, share the highlights of a road trip, bachelorette weekend, or college event—however, nobody needs to hear how many drinks you tossed back with the groom or the extent of the bride's hangover the next morning. Share some laughs with the audience, but not with the intent to overly embarrass the bride or groom.

- **Criticism of the married couple.** It's funny to point out some of the quirks and humorous habits that they may have learned or will soon learn about each other, but it's not your place to project something negative about their future happiness. Make your "Top Five Things

Paul Needs to Know about Anna" list, sure, but leave your list of annoyances about the couple far away from the toast.

- **Over-the-line comments on the physical appearance of one or both of the newlyweds.** You can refer to them as a beautiful couple, or as a stunning bride and handsome groom, but don't use the phrases *smoking hot*, *stone cold fox*, *hunk of meat*, *stud muffin*—you get the idea. Also, no descriptions of bathing suit bodies or bedroom escapades allowed!

WEDDING TOAST WORKOUT:
What Would Nana Think?

Not sure whether something is a toast "don't"? Practice telling the stories, jokes, and/or asides you are considering using in your toast out loud as if you are speaking directly to your parents or grandparents. If you have a full draft of your toast ready, use this exercise when reading it through. Envision your mother, father, grandmother, or grandfather (or all of them!) seated in front of you as you read: Is there a personal story that would have Dad shifting uncomfortably in his seat? A sexual comment that would have Grandma looking for the nearest exit? A joke that would cause Mom to call out your name—first *and* middle—in shock? Ditch it.

Don't Get Intoxicated Beforehand

It is more than fine to enjoy yourself on the special day, but knocking back the booze *before* you make your toast is a dangerous game. Often, what can start out innocently as you wanting to "loosen up" before speaking can quickly lead to you consuming one too many. And once you have reached that point, there is no turning back. If you take the mic while intoxicated, you risk:

- Forgetting lines in your toast
- Exhibiting sloppy or slurred speech
- Saying something you'll regret

And most importantly:

- Making the newlyweds look bad and/or regret choosing you to give a toast on their big day.

The best advice here is to either abstain from any drinks until after your toast *or* set yourself a drink maximum and *stick to it*. Remember: The objective is to honor and entertain loved ones. You can't keep that promise if you're too tipsy to put together clear sentences!

CASE STUDY **Toasting Responsibly**

A few years ago I attended an out-of-town wedding for a good friend. The weekend was a rare opportunity to "get the boys back together." The location was a high-end lake resort, the weather was gorgeous, and the temptation to drink for much of the day before the mid-afternoon ceremony was certainly there. Despite this, the best man had a plan to keep his drinking under control so he could give a great toast and carry out his other best man duties—while still having a good time. He committed to having a maximum of three drinks before the toast (knowing he could operate effectively at this number), and told others about this pledge. Following a drink limit might sound easy, but when you factor in peer pressure, free drinks, nice weather, and several hours of free time, it can actually be quite difficult. By telling others his plan, the best man set clear expectations and garnered our support so that we would back him up if anyone tried to egg him on in drinking more than his limit. He delivered a memorably funny and endearing toast for our longtime friend, the groom, and his new wife.

Don't Make It about You

Your toast is for the married couple first, and for the entertainment of the audience second. Any celebrity status or autograph signings you might envision for yourself are a distant third. Don't worry, though: You'll get lots of satisfaction from the smiles, laughs, and maybe even (happy) tears of the crowd—so the more you can reference the bride and groom, the better. Think of yourself as a supporting character in their movie: Your stories and jokes will help illustrate who they are and how they work as a couple. You want the audience to be focused on and connected to them as much as possible. The minute you present yourself as the "smart one," the "good-looking friend," or the "main event" in the story, you've made yourself the center of attention. If this happens accidentally, or for a fleeting moment, it's no big deal. But if the audience suspects that you're being self-centered, cue the eye-rolls.

Don't Sob Your Way Through It

If you do your toast well, you might be extremely emotional—and that's okay! That type of energy and authenticity will resonate with your audience. Your challenge here will be to contain these supercharged emotions enough to deliver the toast in an effective way.

First, you'll want to avoid rushing through. When people get nervous and/or excited, they tend to speed up: They talk faster, move faster, and are more demonstrative with body language. You'll know you're rushing things if you aren't pausing after each sentence, or you haven't looked up at the audience once in the past thirty seconds. And while a few tears are endearing, if people are struggling to understand you due to consistent crying, you have crossed over into extreme emotions that need to be reined in.

As you are writing your toast, consider mixing your sentimental stories with humorous moments. That way, when you feel yourself getting swept up in your emotions, you can bring yourself back to a more stable, upbeat place to avoid crying. Also, remember that as long as you're holding the microphone, you reserve the right to take a pause and gather your thoughts. At that moment, rather than apologizing, just remain silent as you refocus. The most you should say is, "Excuse me a moment." The audience will understand.

Mapping Out Emotions

The best thing to do up front when it comes to getting emotional is to be aware that it might happen. This way, you can prepare for your feelings ahead of time, and determine whether you are rushing when practicing your toast and also during the main event. Once you've written your first draft, go through and mark what feeling you might have when delivering each part. For example, maybe you have a moving story about how brave the bride is. Mark it with a note like "tears," or a small color-coded circle or dot. Once you see the path your emotions may take as you are giving your toast, you can better plan how to tackle those more overwhelming moments.

If you really need to maintain or regain your composure, speak directly to the bride or groom. This is someone you are comfortable around; it's okay to look directly at them and forget that the audience even exists for a few moments while you brush away tears (or keep them from spilling over). You can also make a quick remark about your emotions, like "These tears are fake, by the way—I'm just a great actor," to lighten the mood and squash any awkwardness. You'll make the married couple laugh, and give yourself that moment to regroup before moving on.

Don't Wing It

You've probably heard someone say, "When I get up there, I'll know what to say." And this may be true...for about 1 percent or less of the population. The vast majority of us, even though we think we might be fine, will struggle to give an impactful speech with little preparation.

The misconception is that giving a speech off the cuff will be more heartfelt and authentic. In reality, these speeches tend to include a lot of pauses, filler words (*uh, umm, you know, I mean*, etc.), and repetition. This is because when your mind inevitably goes blank one moment or you forget a thought along the way, you've got nothing concrete to revert back to.

The best thing you can do is prepare at least the main elements of your toast and then rehearse them as much as possible. In Part 3, you'll learn when to start preparing and rehearsing your toast, so you can nail these fundamentals and even improvise from there if you choose.

WEDDING TOAST WORKOUT:

Taking Note

When you are thinking about the critical elements of your toast, it can be helpful to try automatic writing. Here, you put pen to paper and write whatever pops into your mind, without overthinking, focusing on spelling things correctly, etc. To do this, pull out a piece of paper and write the numbers 1 through 3 vertically down the left-hand side. Use a timer on your phone to give yourself five minutes to write. When the timer starts, jot down the first three stories, topics, etc., that you *absolutely* want to talk about in your toast. When the timer goes off, take a look at what you wrote. Let these three things sit in your mind for a bit before you start fleshing them out for your toast.

Bonus Workout: Besides the three things you wrote on this page, jot down three potential pitfalls that you will actively work to avoid when developing and delivering your toast. These can be related to content you just wrote, your emotional state, body language—anything that came to mind as you read this chapter.

CHAPTER SUMMARY

You've got quite a lot to think about now as you move forward with your toast. Deep breaths! To help you process all of this information, I've provided a quick recap of the main ideas in this chapter—from things you should incorporate in your toast, to those that you shouldn't touch with a ten-foot pole:

- Ditch the inappropriate comments and overly embarrassing stories—no matter how funny they may seem when writing your first draft. It may be helpful to think about these things in terms of what the happy couple typically finds funny, and what they don't. Also, be sure to read the "don'ts" section twice.
- Stay focused on the married couple first, the audience second, and yourself third. You will feel less anxious and come across as more sincere during your toast.
- Preparation won't limit the authenticity of your toast. In fact, it will free up space to improvise while still having a solid leg to stand on.

Part 2

THE FIVE CRITICAL COGS OF A GREAT TOAST

"Cogs"—those little teeth on a gear or wheel—are like the behind-the-scenes workers that no one really gives a lot of credit to but should. Without every cog doing its job, the gear or wheel will not turn, and the larger machine will come to a grinding halt (or just refuse to work in the first place). In the context of a wedding toast, there are essential elements every speech should include: the five "critical cogs" that will set you up for success. First, you've got to grab the audience from the start with a great Opener (after all, they're already gazing at the catering staff and open bar). And then they'll want to hear interesting anecdotes about the bride or groom—the person's past, present, and future. But you'll also need to talk about their significant other. Half the crowd is there because of that person! Lastly, you'll want to end on a glass-clinking high note with a Big Finish.

In this part, you'll learn all about each of the five cogs. You'll explore examples, guiding questions, and unique ways of checking off each cog in your own speech. You'll also take a look at some things to avoid when it comes to those stories about the bride or groom (e.g., embarrassing puberty anecdotes do not pass "Go").

CHAPTER 3

Overview and Cog One: The Opener

I f you want to deliver an entertaining, meaningful, and ultimately memorable toast (of course you do—that's why you're here!), the five critical cogs are your ticket. Why "critical"? Because they are that important! This is a big day for the happy couple, and while there is no one "formula" for the perfect toast, using these five critical cogs will help you give a toast worthy of this occasion. From an Opener that silences even the rowdiest guests, to the stories that perfectly capture the bride or groom as a person and loved one, these essential elements include everything you'll need.

In this chapter you'll get a brief overview of each of the cogs. Then you'll go deeper into the first critical cog: the Opener. Here, you'll find insights and examples to help you create a great Opener for your own dynamite toast. So let's dive in!

THE COGS

By now you've heard a bit about the five "critical cogs" and the important role they will play in the success of your wedding toast. But what exactly *are* they? No need to get restless (love the enthusiasm though!); the following is a quick summary of each cog:

1 **The Opener:** that first powerful line (or few lines) that hooks the audience. For example: a funny or memorable story, relevant quote, or well-timed joke.
2 **The Past:** stories from the past that encapsulate the bride or groom. These memories will make even those long-lost cousins feel close to them.
3 **The Present and Future:** a brief look at where the bride or groom is now—how they have evolved as you've known them, and what lies ahead now that they are entering a new chapter in their lives.
4 **The Significant Other:** a story or gesture that brings the other half of the newly wedded couple into your speech. It is their day too!
5 **The Big Finish:** the last thing you say before passing the mic. The best toasts will end on a high note that leaves the audience laughing, tearing up, or even thinking about it days later (in a *good* way). Your finish can be anything from a grand send-off message or emotional reading of a relevant poem to a deadpan delivery of a great joke.

Now, there is *some* room for improvisation within the five (critical!) cogs (to be discussed more in the next section), but using them as your guide will set you up for a successful toast that the happy couple—and their guests—won't soon forget.

🔎 CASE STUDY **The Invisible Significant Other**

Years ago I attended a wedding where the best man provided a toast that was very entertaining—at least for some. Everyone who went to college with the best man and the groom loved his speech; there were humorous stories of their dorm days and an unforgettable parents' weekend, the memory of when he met the groom, and dating misadventures. There was only one problem: The mention of the bride was a fleeting comment about how she warned him not to tell any inappropriate stories during his toast. His toast was entertaining, sure, but it missed the "honoring" component that comes with the third and fourth cogs: the Present and Future, and the Significant Other. The toast didn't include anything about how the bride and groom met, why they belonged together, or even a few words about the future that lay ahead of them. Nostalgia is great, but it is just one piece of the equation. Without the significant other and their relationship with your loved one, the story is far from complete. You'll learn more about the importance of these cogs and how to include them in your toast in Chapters 5 and 6.

Making Them Your Own

You may be thinking that these cogs will hold you back in some way, but as former Navy SEAL Jocko Willink shared in his book *Extreme Ownership*, "Discipline is freedom." Whether in sports, business, teaching, or giving a wedding toast, it's only *after* you have the fundamentals mastered that you can innovate and test boundaries to make something your very own.

Imagine you want to be a hairstylist who is both creative and revolutionary. You have plans for new styles, coloring, and methods that nobody else in the industry has tried. Maybe the concept you've designed includes varying  lengths, with designs that are extreme and yet somehow still appropriate for most professionals to wear in a work setting. But the drawings that you create, visions you dictate to friends and family, and predictions you make about your inventions don't mean a thing if you don't know how to cut hair. If you have great ideas but cannot demonstrate that you won't send someone home looking like a mutant, you won't get very far.

The point is that taking the fundamentals (in this case, the five critical cogs) seriously will build a great foundation for your toast *and* open the door for any additional ideas you may have for giving it your own unique touch.

COG ONE: The Opener

Bang. That's what you want to hear at the end of the first thirty seconds of your toast—well, you won't hear it so much as *feel* it. It takes many forms, and you'll know if and when it happens: an eruption of laughter, a gasp from the crowd, the palpable feeling of their complete and undivided attention directed toward you.

Obviously, this won't happen if you spend that first half-minute explaining who you are or scrolling through notes on your cell phone, pausing to collect your thoughts before every statement. It won't happen if you are already turnt up from drinking Long Island iced teas at the open bar and can't put together a coherent sentence. And it won't happen if you're reading verbatim from a written statement like it's a class presentation.

It *will* happen if you have prepared your Opener ahead of time, wait until you have the attention of the whole room, speak clearly into the microphone, and slowly pan your eyes across the reception hall confidently as you do. And you *will* be confident, because you'll have thought out your words beforehand, practiced them, and maybe even shared them with a trusted friend or family member for feedback.

Popping the Top Off Your Opener

Not sure where to start when looking for your own "wow factor" Opener? Here's an easy exercise to try! First, look at the following four topics, then use the guiding questions to brainstorm your own examples of each. It may help to write down answers on a separate piece of paper as you go, so you don't forget a thought:

- **Imitation.** Think about the best wedding toast you've ever heard. Come on; really think! How did that person start? Is there a theme, line, or even impactful word that you can borrow and modify for your own Opener? If so, write it down.
- **Joke.** What makes you laugh when you think about the bride or groom? It could be an inside joke (that will still be enjoyed by the rest of the audience) or a hilarious memory. It may need some wordsmithing when it comes to a polished Opener for your toast, but there could be gold here!
- **Childhood memory.** If you've known the bride or groom since childhood, what stands out? Have they come a looooong way from the person you knew as a kid to the

person now making this lifelong commitment? Have they mostly remained the same, albeit taller? What would the audience what to know that you have the special chance to share with them?

- **Quote.** Does either the bride or groom have a favorite quote that you're aware of? Do *you* have a favorite quote that might be relevant to this big day or the happy couple? It could also be a parody of a quote (or song, if you want to get even *more* creative), for a funny twist. Hey, you could be the next "Weird Al" Yankovic—even if just for a moment!

The payoff for your preparation will be huge. Not only will you grab the attention of your audience right from the beginning, but you'll also be setting a great tone for the rest of the toast. After all, the last thing you want is people sneaking off to the hotel bar for tequila shots halfway through, accidentally slamming the door on their way out. *Awkward.*

Sample Openers

To really get the best idea for how to create your own perfect Opener, it is helpful to look at real examples of great Openers. The following are two Openers that captivated the wedding guests and set the stage for successful toasts. Of course, each Opener is subjective to that particular wedding and couple, so remember to tailor yours to your own audience.

DAN THE LION KING

This Opener was part of an all-rhyming toast made by the brother of the groom:

> Good evening, everyone. I am Dan's younger brother Pete.
> Many of you I already know; some I have yet to meet.
>
> Dan and Kate, thank you so much for this wonderful chance—
> by the way, I call first dance.
>
> *people started to boo in jest* What? Sorry, I *called* it!
>
> I've looked up to Dan ever since I've had sight.
> He was always bigger than me, and he was always right.
>
> Being the oldest of four boys couldn't have been an easy thing.
> But in a house full of hyenas, Dan was the lion king.

What worked about this Opener was that it had a mysterious element. After the first two lines rhymed, the audience wondered whether it was a coincidence or the start of a poem. And by the next two lines, they realized it was the latter. Now, the speaker had people hooked on hearing how he would go about fitting each line together in this fun rhyme that also painted a coherent *and* descriptive picture of the groom, his bride, and the occasion—and how exactly the groom deserved the impressive title of "lion king."

BRIAN AND THE RECURRING QUESTION

This Opener began a more traditional toast I wrote for a longtime friend (the groom) and his bride:

> Good evening, ladies and gentlemen.
>
> My name is Pete and I've been a friend of Brian's for more than twenty years.
>
> As I was preparing this toast, one question consistently rang in my mind: How do I summarize a friendship that has lasted since we were in kindergarten? Believe it or not, Brian was under six feet tall then—
>
> *pause for laughter*
>
> But really, how can I possibly speak to all of our experiences in just a few minutes, without it turning into one big inside joke?

While a more classic approach to a wedding toast, this Opener contained two elements that set up the speaker for success. First, he announced that he would *not* be turning the whole speech into an inside joke—something that is common in a lot of toasts made by good friends and family members, and leaves the rest of the audience feeling like outsiders. Instead, in this case, the toaster would be speaking to the crowd in a way that could help them better understand the groom through his unique perspective and experiences.

Second, he posed a question that the rest of the speech would aim to answer: a clear objective for the audience to follow as he continued his toast.

WEDDING TOAST WORKOUT:

Choosing Your Opener

If you completed the previous Wedding Toast Workout in this chapter, you have some content to work with now. But which excerpt from this activity jumps off the page as the perfect Opener for your toast? Start by reading the ideas you brainstormed out loud. Which lines made you smile, laugh, or even tear up? Your Opener is one of these!

If you're still not sure, try this: Reread each excerpt and give it a score from 1 to 10. A score of 1 means you feel nothing when you say it aloud; a 10 makes you laugh out loud, or drives you to tears. Be brutally honest in your scores, and consider only an 8 or above as your Opener. If nothing is higher than a 7, consider taking another stab at the previous Wedding Toast Workout. Trust me: You'd rather make changes now than on the fly when a room full of people is staring at you.

CHAPTER SUMMARY

With these insights and examples at your disposal, you're ready to knock your Opener out of the park! This is your first impression, your golden opportunity to command the crowd so that their undivided attention is appropriately directed toward the happy couple. To make sure this happens, remember to:

- Think about what sticks out to you when you reflect on the bride or groom (or both). Consider memories, relevant jokes, or quotes—anything that comes to mind.
- Make it your own. Borrowing from other resources is fine, but don't be afraid to customize it to the unique relationship between the happy couple, and your own relationship with them.
- Maintain command over the room. If you need to pause until people quiet down before you say your Opener, do it. It's your stage, and the better everyone can hear you, the more you will be able honor the newlyweds.

CHAPTER 4

Cog Two: The Past

Think about your favorite times with the bride or groom. Maybe they involve a family holiday gathering or reunion, hilarious college escapades, or the blood, sweat, and tears of a team sport. These "blasts from the past" are a critical part of your relationship with that person—the special, maybe even transformative moments that bond you. Sharing these stories isn't just fun; it also creates a deeper connection between your audience and the people you are reminiscing about.

And that's where the second cog, the Past, comes in! In this chapter you will further explore how these stories of bygone times with the bride or groom (or both!) will enhance your toast. You'll take your own walk down memory lane to dig up the most unforgettable moments with your loved one. You may find yourself smiling, laughing—even getting a little teary (we won't tell!) as you flip through old photo albums, journal entries, and more. Ready to jump in?

SHARING FOND MEMORIES

There are certain situations that become cornerstones of your life: fundamental building blocks of both who you are and who you become as time goes on. The same is true for the happy couple you will soon be celebrating, and as someone close to them, you have the unique privilege of sharing some of these pivotal memories. In fact, you definitely should, because they will serve as the foundational "soil" from which your wedding toast grows! It is through these stories of the past that you will paint a picture of the bride or groom, connecting them on a deeper level to the audience in ways that only you can.

WEDDING TOAST WORKOUT:
Pondering the Past

A great way to start thinking about your past with the bride or groom is to write things out as you reflect. As you write, you'll probably think of more tidbits that shed light on that person and your bond with them. Having writer's block? Ask yourself these questions to get the ball rolling:

- When did the two of you meet?
- What story or stories do you talk about most when you hang out?

- What quirk(s) do they possess?
- Why are they so important to you? Jot down the answers to some or all of these questions, and don't worry about writing in complete sentences or keeping things in any sort of order.

It may be so subtle that it goes unnoticed, but your perspective on the bride or groom is a link between them and all of the wedding guests—especially those who are closer to the other half of the happy couple. After all, this special day is all about bringing people together!

CASE STUDY **Maybe Leave the Cooking to the Chef**

One maid of honor used her initial brainstorming about the bride's quirks to tell a story that both painted a more vivid picture of the bride and her relationship with the groom, and also segued perfectly into the fourth cog, the Significant Other (you will learn more about this cog in Chapter 6).

She talked about meeting the bride, Emily, at a cooking class a few years before the big day. Emily had quite a few hilarious incidents throughout the class, including starting a small fire. From there, Emily's skills only barely improved—much to the chagrin of her friends and family. Luckily, the groom happened to be a full-time chef. A perfect match! The maid of honor delivered the story flawlessly, and everyone shared a good laugh before she moved on to talk more about the groom.

Common Themes

Everyone has unique shared experiences with their loved ones, but there are also a few common themes that can serve as a guide when it comes to deciding which of these experiences to include in your wedding toast:

- **Fondest memories.** What sticks out when you think about that person?
- **Mischief.** What are things you did together that got you into trouble?
- **Fights.** When did you get under each other's skin? Did you learn anything from the experience? Is it something you laugh about now?
- **Fun trips.** Is there something that stands out from a trip you took together? Did a defining moment of your relationship occur during the trip?
- **Growing pains.** If you grew up together, was there anything noteworthy about the person's development during those years? Did you have a fear of the opposite sex, while they were confident? Did they grow seven inches taller in a year?
- **Location-specific anecdotes.** Was there a memorable tree house, friend's basement, swimming pool, classroom, or school dance that produced vivid memories for you both?

CASE STUDY **Grade School Stories**

During one wedding reception, two co-maids of honor shared the microphone for a toast to their good friend, the bride. The three women had met before starting the first grade, and by the wedding day their friend-

ship had spanned more than two decades. The first half of their combined toast included stories of their journey together from primary school through middle and high school. From ages six to eighteen these women were nearly inseparable, and through their tales of school mischief and high school hilarity, the co-maids of honor invited the audience into this special friendship, including them in inside jokes, and generally making everyone feel both a sense of togetherness and a closeness to the bride. Even for just a few minutes, everyone in the crowd felt a part of the bride's story.

Sharing two to three more in-depth memories, or five or six quick recollections, will give your toast that personal, insightful touch without turning it into one big inside story or rambling monologue that has people shifting in their chairs and checking the time.

Automatic Writing, Take 2

If you tried the automatic writing exercise in Chapter 2 (Wedding Toast Workout: Taking Note), you know how helpful it can be in getting all of your jumbled thoughts onto the page so you can root through and organize them more easily. Give it a try here! Take five minutes to write about each of the previous themes. Use a timer and write until it goes off—no overthinking, no stopping to reword clumsy sentences. No one else is going to know that you missed the second *a* in *accidentally*.

CHAPTER SUMMARY

Your past holds more gold than California in 1848: Dig into your memory to mine for those memories and bring them out into the open—and into your toast. Here are a few quick reminders and main takeaways to help you nail this cog in your speech:

- A walk down memory lane will help you during the brainstorming stage of writing your toast. Be sure to use the guiding questions in this chapter.
- The Past cog connects the audience not only to their own fond memories but also to the history of the married couple.
- These insightful stories will also keep the audience more engaged and less likely to become restless or bored during your toast.

CHAPTER 5

Cog Three: The Present and Future

s you've left school, started and possibly changed jobs, and maybe moved, gotten married, or had kids, you've come to understand that your relationships with friends and family members change with every chapter in life. Maybe there are a few bumps in the road as careers take off, families grow and perhaps even move farther away, and you see each other less consistently. After all, life happens! But when someone really matters to you, you still find ways to keep that connection alive—even from a distance.

Okay, so you don't need me to tell you that your bond with the bride or groom (or both) is special, but what you *should* know is that this toast is the perfect chance to celebrate how far that relationship has come, and share your excitement for what the future has in store for them in this new phase of their life. In this chapter you'll explore the present of your relationship with both your loved one and their significant other, the promising future ahead of them, and how mentioning these important elements in your toast is a great and easy way to both honor their relationship and give them your support. Whether it is a life of travel, a settled home with kids, or simply fulfilling their destiny to be together (cue the "aww"s), they've got so much to look forward to...and you get to be that messenger of great news!

EXPLORING THE PRESENT

Whether you met ten years ago or just months or even days ago (okay, probably not *days*), your relationship with the bride or groom has led up to this point—this moment. And it's a big moment! Why *wouldn't* you include it in your toast? This part of cog number three connects where the bride and/or groom have been—and where you've been with them— to where they're going. Your stories about the past got the ball rolling, and now this segue into the present will take you toward home plate.

WEDDING TOAST WORKOUT:
Tracking Positivity

When you have a full draft of your toast, try marking positive versus negative phrases to see how frequent each type is. Use green and red markers to leave a plus or minus sign next to each type so each is easy to spot and you can quickly notice the frequency and any patterns in negative or positive lines. Use this tracker to decide where you might need to make a cut or reword something, or move things around. As a general rule of thumb, you should always sandwich a more negative (even joking) remark between two positive ones.

This cog also honors your loved one, giving them due credit for how far they have come and how much they mean to you. What better place to be sentimental than at a wedding? And speaking of sentiment, close family members, extended relatives, friends, and anyone else at the wedding want to participate in the happiness of the day. By sharing your excitement for this special time, you connect more deeply to your audience through those good vibes!

CASE STUDY **Across the World**

In one wedding toast, the father of the groom segued from his past relationship with his son as his mentor to the bond they had now as peers—and even as a student himself, with his son showing him how to do certain things. He mentioned tying bow ties before the ceremony that morning as an example. In the past he was the teacher, showing his son the ropes in everything from riding a bike to fixing a leaky faucet. That day, however, it was his son's job to teach him, as it had been years since the father had worn a bow tie, and even in the past he had needed to use a diagram to figure out exactly how to tie it. The groom taught him his easy trick for tying a bow tie, and his father was reminded that his son now had his own set of skills to teach, and he was proud to learn from him—that day and in the days to come.

Of course, there are some basic guidelines for what you should consider including in this part of your toast, and what you should avoid:

1 Reflections of your gratitude for how far you've come together to get to this day are a great thing to include.

2 Proclamations that you "cannot believe" you're here, or that you're "surprised" you were "even invited" after all you've "been through" are a no-go. You may acknowledge that your relationship with your loved one has had its ups and downs—as long as you follow that with the happiness you currently share as friends or family members.

3 Finally, it's always a good idea to share why you are proud of this person. If you feel compelled to question their recent decisions or their choice of significant other, it's a conversation to have one-on-one (if you must)—definitely not in front of a crowd of guests on their wedding day. Nothing will undermine your toast more than wading into those treacherous waters, even if you think it will be a funny, tongue-in-cheek moment. Spoiler alert: It won't be.

CASE STUDY **The Present's Presents**

During one wedding reception, the maid of honor gave a toast that knocked this cog out of the park. After walking through her favorite memories with the bride, she transitioned to the present state of their relationship. She talked about the bride's recent move back to her town, how happy that made her, and the fun times they have been able to have now that they spend more time together. After a hilarious recount of her role in the bride and groom's first date, she shared her enthusiasm for them as a couple and the dreams now coming true for them, and her deep gratitude for having her dear friend so actively involved in her life despite how crazy her own life has been. Through her mention of the present and what was in store for her friend, she honored the happy couple and their special day, and connected the audience even more to the bride.

LOOKING AHEAD

The future element of this cog is all about what's in store for the married couple. Where will they go after the cake is gone and the honeymoon tans fade? What will they accomplish together? What experiences will they share? What impact will they have in the world? You aren't putting words into their mouths, but you are affirming your belief in and support of their success as a couple moving forward. For example, you wouldn't say, "I expect them to have three kids and settle down into their hometown while he works as an accountant and she climbs the nursing ladder between pregnancies." Instead, you might say, "Now that their two personalities and talents are fused together, great things are bound to happen. I'm just hoping to ride their coattails for a small percentage of their fortune." Sure, they may not need the encouragement, but it adds an extra dose of love and excitement to your toast, and perfectly ties together the loose ends of your past and present elements.

CASE STUDY **Funny Forecasting**

There is one exception to note here when it comes to making predictions: if you have a great joke or an absurd forecast of the future that you know will get laughs from both the couple and the crowd. For example, one best man and former college basketball teammate of the groom's mentioned how excited he was for them to have ten kids—enough for five-on-five basketball games in the driveway. A maid of honor also pretended that the bride told her about her plans to turn their spare bedrooms, basement, and living room into the site of a crazy business venture.

More than anything, you'll want to drive home the point that the happy couple are and will continue to be great together—and that you plan to be there for them through it all. They can't get rid of you even if they try!

WEDDING TOAST WORKOUT:

Asking Key Questions

When thinking about how to work this cog into your toast, there are a few helpful questions you can ask yourself. In a broader context, honest exploration and discussion of these questions with the bride or groom ahead of time can lead to a healthier and more rewarding relationship with that important person—and their significant other.

- How do you feel about this person now versus in your past interactions?
- What was your reaction when they asked you to speak on this special day in their life?
- How will your interactions with this person shift now that they are married?
- Where do you see your relationship with this person heading?
- What does this couple have the potential to accomplish in their married life?

CHAPTER SUMMARY

The Present and Future cog builds on the foundation of the Past cog to give your audience a well-rounded view of your loved one. It tells their story, starting with nostalgia and finishing with an open-ended optimism for this next chapter in their life. Below are a few important things to keep in mind as you include the present and future in your toast:

- Your perspective on the present enhances this special day. Use it as an opportunity to pump even more excitement into the room.
- Your relationship with the bride or groom (or both) is constantly evolving, and it's okay to admit that. Make a commitment to continue supporting your loved one through thick and thin.
- Make sure your present and future remarks are mostly positive. If you mention a difficult situation you faced with the bride or groom, sandwich it between two more upbeat anecdotes.

CHAPTER 6

Cog Four: The Significant Other

No matter how close you are to the bride or groom—how long you have known them, or how deep your bond goes—it is crucial that you also talk about their new husband or wife in your toast. After all, it's their big day too! And they clearly mean a lot to your loved one. So it's important to show due respect by celebrating them and their major part in the occasion—as tempting as it may be to focus on all of those great memories you share with the bride or groom.

This chapter is your roadmap to effectively honoring the significant other in your own wedding toast. You'll discover helpful exercises for brainstorming what to include, as well as a few major things to avoid. You'll also find examples of some of these big "don'ts" in action. And at the end of the section you'll explore some easy tips for talking to the happy couple about your toast, from what things you may plan to include, to what they might want you to avoid mentioning.

IT TAKES TWO

It's worth repeating: It is the significant other's special day too. This occasion wouldn't even be *happening* without them—and your loved one certainly wouldn't be gearing up for a new, exciting chapter in life if it weren't for them.

To truly celebrate the day and the happy couple with your toast, you will need a tasteful transition from the stories about the bride or groom to their significant other. The key to doing this well is striking the right balance between humor, intrigue, and respectfulness. If your mention of the significant other is cliché, bland, or more like an afterthought, it will come off as boring, forgettable, or worse: insincere. And if you belly flop into this portion of your toast by mentioning, say, the "hotness" of the bride or the "stupidity" of the groom, you are in for an awkward next few days (probably more, actually). Instead, include a well thought-out acknowledgment that celebrates that person and welcomes them to this awesome new adventure with your loved one. It can be funny, meaningful, or both. You can include things like the first thing the bride or groom told you about them; something funny the couple share together (both love the same movie, neither can cook, they root for rival sports teams, etc.); or examples of how she keeps the groom on his toes, how he supports her through thick and thin, or how they perfectly complement each other. Keep it relatively brief, while still paying the respect the significant other deserves.

The Significance of the Other

Not sure what to include in your mention of the significant other? Start by asking yourself these questions:

- How did the couple meet?
- Have you had any memorable interactions with the significant other?
- Does the couple have any inside jokes that you're aware of?
- What kinds of things is the significant other into?
- Does the bride or groom have any quirks that the significant other loves (or doesn't)?

Things to Avoid

In addition to those great insights you can provide, there are some things to keep *out* of your toast when talking about the significant other. Avoid mentioning any of the following, unless you want things to get uncomfortable fast:

- A negative first impression of the significant other.
- Anything that you think is weird or "off" about them.

- A personal or family quirk they might not want discussed in public (e.g., that his uncle is a conspiracy theorist, her dad doesn't know about her tattoos, or his cousin is in prison).
- Anything remotely related to your opinion of their attractiveness. Even if you think it's a funny line—even if the world is ending on the following Monday—skip it.

CASE STUDY **Rules for Marrying My Friend**

In one toast, a maid of honor followed her introduction to the crowd with a laundry list of rules for the groom to abide by if he was to be worthy of a life with her friend, the bride. Now, I'm all for giving pointers or advice for a happy marriage, but the tone of her toast came off as demanding and condescending toward the significant other. Always keep in mind as you write and give your toast that just like your loved one, the significant other is to be honored and entertained, not lectured. It's a big day for them—why put a damper on it? In this case, many of us in the crowd were left scratching our heads and wondering, *Was she serious about the rules? What will she do if he doesn't follow them?* Not the impression you want to leave your audience with.

PREPPING THE COUPLE

Now that you have a better idea of what to include in your toast and what is probably best to keep to yourself, it's time for an important and often overlooked task: preparing the happy couple for your toast.

Of course, the wedding day is the most important day of their lives (well, one of the most important at least). And after all of the money, planning, dress and suit fittings, cake tastings, and rehearsals, they want the day to be perfect. So, putting yourself in their shoes here, you can imagine that they might be a little anxious about the toasts—after all, the horror stories and hilariously uncomfortable movie scenes are endless.

While initially it might seem outrageous to tell a toaster what shouldn't be said, what jokes shouldn't be used, etc., it does make sense the more you think about it. An incendiary line, hurtful shots at someone's family, or excessive stories of drunken stupidity can really cast a shadow on the entire event.

Walking the line of appropriateness—or leaping over it—is not a way to honor the happy couple. In fact, it makes the toast more about you and your desire to get laughs than about them. Always remember that the point of this is to honor and entertain the married couple first, the crowd second, and yourself third.

🔍 CASE STUDY **The "Epic Vacation" Story**

You probably have fond memories of a road trip, beach day, or international vacation with friends or family members. I can relate: Some of the best times of my life took place on the beaches of South Carolina and California, in the pools and casinos of Las Vegas, and on the narrow streets of New Orleans' French Quarter. And I have no qualms about including a mention of a favorite trip in your toast. However, when the best man at one reception dove into a story about an "epic trip with the guys," it was a classic example of crossing the line into inappropriate material for a wedding toast. The crowd didn't need to know details about the women they met (especially since none of them was the bride), the drinking games they played, or the "secrets" about the groom that the best man alluded to. His summary of a trip that included "a lot of firsts for us and definitely many things we can never tell our wives" proved not only alienating for most of the guests in the audience but also very awkward for the groom, his bride, and everyone else to hear.

With all of this in mind, the best way to give the marrying couple peace of mind and ensure that you are not about to create an awkward or even tense situation with your toast is by discussing it with them ahead of time. You don't have to show your full hand here, but you should cover anything you might be unsure about, and anything they feel you should know, before raising a glass on the big day. To help you out with this conversation, here are three promises you can make to the couple. This also serves as a great reminder of what not to do as you give your toast:

- **Don't be downright mean.** If something you say is funny and good-natured but someone takes offense, it is on them. Hey, you can't please everyone! So focus on pleasing the bride and groom. However, if you have an axe to grind with somebody in the room and you think this is the perfect chance to knock them down a peg, think again. There's no place for mean comments in your toast, and the bride and groom will be very happy to hear you say so.
- **Don't be sexually suggestive.** It's never as funny to others as it may be to you.
- **Don't divulge any stories or personal information they would rather not be shared with the crowd.** Be sure to ask them outright if there is anything they want kept under wraps.

These promises take very little effort on your end, and simply communicating them to the bride and groom will help put their minds at ease. After hearing these promises and discussing anything that they want kept off the record, they are likely to give you their blessing to write the toast as you see fit.

In some cases, however, a bride or groom may still want to see your full toast in advance. While it may feel as though they don't trust you to follow through on your promises and any requests they may have, remember that it is more about their day than about you. Weddings are exciting, but they can also be very stressful and nerve-wracking. The couple just wants to be sure everything goes off without a hitch.

CHAPTER SUMMARY

Marriage is an equal partnership, and this special day belongs to both people. To ensure that the significant other is included in your toast—and in the best ways—remember the following key ideas from this chapter:

- Shoot for a 70/30 ratio in your toast content: 70 percent on your loved one and 30 percent on the significant other. You may not reach this exact percentage, but using it as your guide will be helpful.
- Share your unique perspective on your loved one as a person since meeting the significant other. You've seen their interactions from a different angle than most, so share this to give the crowd a more well-rounded experience.
- Avoid sharing any embarrassing story or inside joke that the bride or groom will be ashamed to have to explain to people afterward.

CHAPTER 7

Cog Five: The Big Finish

The best speeches, regardless of occasion, end on a high note. From the final, drawn-out *E* of an opera to the long-awaited resolution at the end of a movie, the finale is what people remember most. You want to leave your audience with a big smile, a round of applause, and maybe even their jaws hanging open.

In this chapter you'll explore how to make that happen with the fifth and final cog: the Big Finish! Here, you'll match the best kind of finish to your own unique toast. Whether you choose a tear-inducing welcome to the family, a joke that has everyone clutching their sides, or a cheer that leads to a standing ovation, your Big Finish is sure to be part of the happy couple's cherished memories.

FINDING YOUR FINISH

"Big Finish" sounds a little intimidating, but don't worry; it's actually pretty simple to execute. When you are writing your toast, save your best story, your best joke, or your most defining moment with the couple for the end. Simple enough! Let yourself get emotional, or deliver that killer punchline with confidence, then wait for the house to come down.

🔍 CASE STUDY **The Bear and His Honey**

I used the following Big Finish in my toast at my brother Dan's wedding. The idea came when I was identifying the key things I wanted to accomplish in my Big Finish: to tie my past with my brother to the present and future, include the significant other (my sister-in-law, Kate), and do it all in rhyme (this finish was for an all-rhyming toast). To accomplish this, I thought about something I could pull from our childhood, and whether it could be used to wish them well as they started their married life together. I remembered that Dan's nickname was "the Bear" when we were kids, and my Big Finish hit me like a thunderbolt. You can find the full toast in the Appendix:

> I'm proud of Dan, and really happy to officially welcome
> Kate to our family.
> You know, it's kind of funny:
> Dan's nickname growing up was "the Bear"…and this bear
> has found his honey.

The final line definitely ended my toast and transitioned me into raising my glass—and signaled the crowd to follow suit—in a champagne toast to the happy couple. The applause and cheers from this Big Finish have inspired me as I've gone on to write and deliver other speeches.

By now you have explored activities and tips in previous chapters that will help you find your best stories, jokes, and touching acknowledgments of the newlyweds. From there it's just a matter of saving the very best for last. If you are still looking for your Big Finish, revisit these exercises with that ultimate goal in mind. You can also check out more examples online or talk things over with a close friend or family member to get their insight.

Things to Remember

Of course, there are also a few "don'ts" to keep in mind when it comes to your Big Finish. You've probably seen it before, maybe at another wedding, a graduation ceremony, or another big event: the finale that falls flat, feels forced, or just doesn't seem to fit with the rest of the person's speech. Maybe they started to doubt their words and cut things short so they could get out of the spotlight ASAP, or they went for a tired cliché that took away some of the sincerity of their words. It happens. But if you keep their "don'ts" in mind as you write and deliver your Big Finish, you can avoid it happening to *you*:

- Don't use a cliché—unless it really, *really* fits with a main story, joke, or sentiment you used previously in the toast.

- Don't rush through it. You should have planned the timing of your toast before the big day, so unless something completely unexpected happens, there is no reason to hurry. If you notice that you are talking a bit too fast or getting nervous during your Big Finish, take a beat to regroup and slow things down. Mark a spot in your Big Finish where this pause can happen if needed.
- Don't completely wing it. You might be hit with a better Big Finish as you are giving your toast and that's fine, but don't plan to just "figure something out" when you get up there.

🔍 CASE STUDY **Winging It**

One maid of honor gave a toast that didn't have a Big Finish at all. After talking about her past with the bride and how she met the groom, she started to trail off. Not only did the toast feel incomplete, but it left the audience wondering whether they should clap or wait for her to possibly say more. What was worse was that the maid of honor seemed to realize this in the moment, and tried to wing a Big Finish. Because she hadn't prepared ahead of time and was now nervous, the ending she threw together was generic (essentially just an "I love you" to the happy couple), felt disconnected from the rest of the toast, and was full of "um"s and "uh"s.

Your Movie Mic-Drop Moment

When creating your Big Finish, it may also help to think about the structure of a movie. Most movies have an introduction, where the characters are introduced and some kind of backstory is presented. Then a series of events leads to a defining point in the story: the climax. For your toast, the first four cogs lead up to this climactic moment (a.k.a. the Big Finish). The audience will stay engaged through your whole toast when they sense that you're heading for a climax—so give the people what they want!

In your toast this climax might be a one-liner, a quote that is meaningful to you and the bride or groom, a story that proves to you why this marriage is destined for success, or a heartfelt message that leaves no dry eyes in the venue. The climax will depend on the path you have taken in your own unique toast, so let your imagination lead you!

TYING EVERYTHING TOGETHER

While it *is* called the Big *Finish*, there is one final thing to include in your toast once the applause has died down. When wrapping things up, you should also spend a moment giving thanks for this great opportunity you were given. After all, the newlyweds picked you out of everyone to have a special voice on this important day. After delivering your Big Finish and allowing time for the audience to react, simply add a genuine thank you to the bride and groom. This will also ensure that the focus is back on them as everyone raises their glasses.

CHAPTER SUMMARY

This is the Big Finish for your big toast. Spend the time to get it right, but don't overthink it. Here are the key things to remember when it comes to nailing your movie mic-drop moment:

- Start by thinking about the reaction you're looking for from the crowd. This will give you direction in deciding whether you want to go for a joke or funny story, or a more sentimental line.
- There is no one perfect way to end your toast. The best Big Finishes are custom-fitted to that specific happy couple. You know these two people—use that to your advantage!
- Practice your choreography. How are you going to move from saying the final lines, to raising your glass, to turning over the mic? No awkward half-raises or side-hugs allowed!

Part 3

YOUR TOAST TOOLBOX

By now you've read through different tips and tricks, traveled down memory lane, looked to the future, and given more thought to the significant other. You've got the five critical cogs down and have probably done some brainstorming along the way—or even polished some of the stories, jokes, or sentimental remarks you are going to use in your toast. Now it's time to bring everything home!

This part is your personal toolbox for creating and executing your own fantastic wedding toast. You'll read insights into presentation and managing a toast with more than one speaker or the addition of guest speakers. You'll also find a full checklist of tasks and deadlines for writing, polishing, and practicing your toast, so you can avoid that pesky urge to procrastinate (it entices the best of us!). With these tools at your disposal, you will be ready to bring your full wedding toast to life *and* deliver it successfully.

CHAPTER 8

Presentation Matters

It doesn't take a fashion icon to know that presentation is important when it comes to giving your toast. Looking disheveled, muttering or mumbling, or staring at the floor will only take away from the impact of your words. Even if you have crafted the most amazing speech on planet Earth, the wedding guests won't be able to focus on what you are saying if your shirt has a gigantic stain on it—or you aren't wearing a shirt at all. And that's just the tip of the iceberg: There are a lot of little ways that you can look your best (or not-so-best) when taking that mic to address the crowd.

Luckily, this chapter is here to help! Here, you will discover easy ways to give your best performance, no matter how nervous you might be feeling on the inside. You'll also look at examples of what not to do and how those seemingly innocent actions can take away from the impact of even the most brilliant wedding toast.

GIVING A GREAT PERFORMANCE

Maybe you've never given a speech before and have absolutely no idea what to do once all eyes are on you. Maybe it's been a while since you've raised a glass and need a few pointers or refreshers. Or maybe you are looking for some reassurance to calm your nerves around talking in front of an audience. Regardless of your public speaking skills (or lack thereof), you've come to the right place. The following are quick and easy tips for giving a great performance deserving of your great toast. Be sure to work in some time before the big day to practice these techniques, even if just in front of a mirror.

- Stand up straight with your chest slightly out. You're up there for a reason and should be proud of that. Stand proud, and eventually you'll *feel* proud.
- When you get the microphone, take a full three seconds to survey the crowd before you speak. This will build intrigue in the room as people anticipate what you're about to say. It also provides time for you to gather your thoughts.

Breathe In, Breathe Out

It can feel really uncomfortable and even challenging for some people to take that pause before speaking in front of a crowd. You might feel like three seconds drags on for twenty—like the audience is wondering what is taking so long, why you haven't gotten the show on the road yet. Plus, the sooner you start, the sooner you'll be done, right? Okay, maybe so, but remember: This isn't about being done ASAP—it's about honoring the newlyweds on their big day. And that pause is your perfect moment to take command of the crowd and squash any nerves so you can do it well.

If you find when practicing your toast that you are still struggling to leave space for that pause, it may help to pair it with a quick breathing exercise or silent, affirming mantra that fills it for you and kicks any awkwardness you might be feeling about this silence to the curb. When practicing your toast, try taking a deep breath in through your nose as you count to two. Then exhale slowly as you count one more beat. Or try saying this easy mantra to yourself during your pause: "I have an important message, and I'm excited to share it." When you are done, start your toast.

- Look at the audience more than you look at your speech. It's fine to look down and read off of the page once in a while as you give your toast; however, don't completely ignore the people you are actually speaking to.

🔍 CASE STUDY **Wow, Those Shoes Look Great**

During one toast, the speaker spent the better part of ten minutes admiring her shoes as she talked. It made it difficult to concentrate on what she was saying, as everyone was distracted by what was so interesting about her heels. Don't get me wrong; I appreciate a nice pair of shoes as much as the next person. But when it comes to a toast, a major lack of eye contact with the audience prevents them from truly connecting with what you're saying. It also takes away from the feeling behind your words. Maybe you are going for a really moving story about your friendship with the bride, but because you are not looking at anyone as you talk about it, no one knows how emotional this moment actually is for you—or how *they* should feel about it. Had this speaker simply paused every thirty seconds or so to look up at the crowd, or even just make eye contact with the married couple as she talked about them, the toast could have been a success.

- Give yourself a quick look and sweep of the hand to make sure you don't have any crumbs or stains on your clothes, or toilet paper stuck to your shoe. These can be very distracting to people in the audience.

CASE STUDY **The TP Bandit**

During one toast, the father of the bride had an impressive train of toilet paper attached to his shoe. How he made it to the stage without anyone tipping him off is a mystery, but there he was—and, frankly, it was pretty distracting. As much as people wanted to listen to his stories and jokes, it was hard to look away from the toilet paper, and no one wanted to make it potentially worse by interrupting the toast to point it out. While it made for a funny memory later, it also made for an *un*memorable toast. Check your shoes after using the bathroom—this is good advice no matter where you are!

- Hold the microphone close enough to your mouth. A lot of people may say not to "swallow the mic," and you definitely should avoid doing this, but in the end, it's better to be too loud than not loud enough. Don't prevent anyone in the back of the room from hearing your toast. It's perfectly fine to ask the audience, "Can everyone hear me?" if you are unsure.

CASE STUDY **The Low Talker**

I've seen countless best men, maids of honor, fathers of the bride, and other wedding speakers fail to establish a good volume when giving their toast. The most common perpetrator is the holds-the-mic-like-a-TV-remote speaker. They grip the mic closer to the bottom and wave it around as they speak (and not necessarily in the direction of their mouth). The crowd hears about one third of their words as they swing the mic back and forth as if trying to change channels on an invisible TV. Of course, they aren't doing it on purpose, and sometimes a bold crowd member might shout, "We can't hear you," but by that time the speaker is halfway through a thought and everything is thrown off.

Always keep the mic right in front of your mouth while talking. It may seem like common sense, but it can be a whole different ballgame when all of the lights, eyes, and ears are on you. If possible, test the waters before the big day—especially if you've never used a mic before.

Additional Resources

If you feel that you need more resources on the presentation aspect of your toast (hey, it can be pretty nerve-wracking!), by all means pursue it. Body language, verbal cues, and visual appearance are all things that you can learn more about through online videos, articles, books, and even discussions with friends or family members. Every little bit of extra effort will go a long way in both easing any anxiety you might have about the toast and setting you up for success when the big day rolls around.

WEDDING TOAST WORKOUT:

Self-Awareness

If you've struggled with public speaking in the past, are currently feeling nervous about giving your wedding toast, or are already comfortable with the spotlight and just want to improve your skills, here's an exercise in self-awareness that can help! This easy body language check will make you aware of how you are holding different parts of your body, so you can adjust in ways that better convey confidence and get your message across to the audience. Start by asking yourself the questions for each of the following elements as you practice your toast, then use the instructions for better posture.

If you use this exercise consistently while practicing, it can become a habit that carries over into other public speaking situations too:

1. **Head.** Is your chin pointed downward toward the floor? Is your head fixed in one place while speaking? Tilt your chin up to face forward at eye level, and slowly move your head from left to right as you talk. This will allow you to connect with as many people as possible, and project your voice clearly across the room.

2. **Hands.** You've got one hand on the mic—where is the other hand? Is it behind your back? On your hip? Is it shaking? If you are holding a piece of paper or phone as you give your toast, you are covered. But if you find your hand shaking, try moving it a bit as you talk. It will help animate what you are saying, while hiding the trembling that is more noticeable when your hand is held in one place. If you aren't holding anything, still move your hand at least once in a while during your toast to give your words more energy. When not moving it, you can keep it at your side, but avoid putting it on your hip or behind your back. Having a hand on your hip subconsciously relays impatience to both the crowd and yourself. Having it behind your back conveys less confidence in your words.

3 **Feet.** How are your feet positioned—close together or far apart? Toes pointing in or out? Standing with your feet slightly farther than shoulder-width apart, toes pointed either straight ahead or slightly out, will project confidence and help you avoid leaning or tripping. You can also walk around as you talk to give your toast more energy and spread your attention evenly across a larger audience. Just be sure to watch for electrical cords or chairs, to avoid tripping, and long table linens, so you don't pull them down onto the floor with you (like I did at a conference once).

Repeat "head, hands, feet" to yourself when practicing your toast to easily remember to check the placement of these three important body parts.

CHAPTER SUMMARY

Maybe you're starting to feel a bit nervous now, and that's okay! Why? Because with your dynamite toast and the presentation tips in this chapter, you've got this. So when it's time to take the mic, just remember:

- A well-written toast is half the battle, but your presentation matters too. Look the part.
- Eye contact with the crowd is critical in establishing an emotional connection during your toast.
- "Head, hands, feet" will help you simplify and control your body language.

CHAPTER 9

Group Toasts and Guest Speakers

What if you're not the only one giving the toast? Or what if you decide that your story about the first time you met the groom would be better told with the help of another friend? Group toasts and guest speakers are a great way to enhance the experience: more unique perspectives, more laughs—more tears, if you're taking the emotional route. And if you choose to enlist other speakers, or the bride or groom decides they want multiple people (e.g., siblings or childhood friends) to toast together, it's best to be prepared. Remember how badly group projects went in school when you all decided to just wing it? The same will happen here if you don't take the time to plan things out ahead of time.

This chapter is here to help you with this preparation. Here, you'll explore what to expect with a group toast or guest speakers, as well as important things to consider, from independent versus group brainstorming, to who says what—and when. You'll learn how to work together and be proactive in order to create and execute a truly memorable toast.

A PARTY OF TWO (OR MORE)

If you do decide to give a toast with someone else (or a group of people), or the bride or groom makes the decision for you (deep breaths—it's their day, and you will successfully navigate this!), there are a few things to think about. You've got your different (maybe even conflicting) ideas, any schedule issues when getting together with the other people in the group, and so on. It's certainly different from an individual toast. One important note: If the bride or groom *has* decided on a group toast, remember that this is not a rivalry. They chose this path because they wanted to show equal love to all of you.

Now, before jumping into that brainstorming stage, there are a couple of different routes you can take when writing a group toast:

1 Brainstorm and take notes independently, then come together to create a toast (or multiple partial toasts, one for every person who will be speaking). This may work best if you have busy or conflicting schedules, or if you work better alone.

2 Brainstorm, share notes, and write the toast (or partial toasts) together. This route can lead to some great additions you may not have generated on your own.

🔍 CASE STUDY **The Triple Threat**

A close friend of mine had two co-best men for his wedding, and they gave me a small role as a third speaker in their toast. We decided to meet up in person twice during the writing process. For the first meeting, we brought our own individual notes for what we wanted to include. Most of this meeting was spent sharing these notes, as well as anything else we thought of as we talked. The best men had the final say, but they took my opinions into consideration while choosing which anecdotes made the cut. Together, we decided what I would say during my time slot and about how long it would take. At the second meeting, the best men had made a full draft of their toast, and we decided where my lines would come in. We also practiced the full toast a few times, working out the specifics of where I would be sitting in relation to the stage before I got up to take the mic, when I would come to the stage, and how I would shift attention back to the best men after I was done. Because we met beforehand and communicated effectively, the writing process was seamless and the speech received a lot of laughs (and a few sniffles) from the crowd—especially the married couple.

Working Together

After you've decided which route works best for you and the other toaster(s), you'll want to come up with a game plan that keeps everyone up to speed, on task, and ready to make that wedding deadline. To help you out, I've provided an overview of the key things your game plan should include:

- A set date and time to get together, either virtually or in person. Aim for two meetings minimum: the first to create a rough draft of the toast, and the second to polish it and practice everyone's speaking parts.
- Expectations for what everyone needs to bring to each meeting.
- One designated person to take notes during the meetings, write out the full rough draft during or following the first meeting, and create the polished final draft during the second meeting. This can be multiple people.

Your game plan should also include specifics for what will happen during each meeting. Important tasks for your game plan are:

- Reading through everyone's notes during the first meeting
- Deciding which stories, jokes, and other remarks to include in the toast, and which to veto
- Building a chronological framework for the toast

Making the Toast

Once you've created your game plan, met with the other toaster(s), and polished your final toast, it's important to practice a smooth delivery so you'll be sure to knock it out of the park when the big day finally arrives. You're first going to want a clear understanding of who talks when. During your last meeting it may be helpful to have each person pick one or two comments, jokes, or stories from the polished toast that they absolutely want to deliver. Then you can divvy up the remaining lines.

Then, once the speaking parts have been sorted out, you can use one of the following simple strategies to deliver those lines, or create your own—whatever works for your group:

- Write the toast on notecards, with each change in speaker beginning a new card. Be sure to number the cards in the order they will be read. Each speaker can have a full set of these cards, or mark on their own cards what phrase comes right before it's their turn to talk.
- Color-code all copies of the toast so each speaker's lines are in a specific color.
- Establish a nonverbal cue that every person will use to let the next speaker know it's their turn. A head nod, point in their direction, or other introductory hand gesture will work.

And remember: Multiple people on the microphone does not equal creative license to put on a twenty-minute show. Keep everyone's speaking part(s) to a reasonable length that does not add up to any more than ten total minutes.

WHAT IF THEY SLACK OFF?

Thanks to those "fun" group projects in school, you know that sometimes (okay, most of the time) not everyone is going to pull their weight. As frustrating as that can be when you're just trying to create a great toast for your loved one's special day, all you can do is prepare, prepare, and prepare. Once you've done your part and you've devised what you're going to say during the toast, your conscience is clean.

It may also help ease any worries if you work out a game plan for how you would handle the other person (or people) not having their part(s) done in time, dropping out of the toast altogether, or forgetting their copy of the toast at home. For example, if you know your partner is a procrastinator, it may be helpful to check in with them every week just to see how their progress is coming along. You can even provide this person with bullet points that summarize their segments of the toast, so they just have to turn the bullets into a narrative. The more clarity you can provide and the easier you make it for the other person, the more likely it will be done well and on time. If you do have a reasonable doubt that a person in your group toast will even stick through to the big moment, it won't hurt to have filler stories, jokes, or other remarks to take up that space and time—or a segue from the lines before their part to the lines following, so the gap isn't even noticed by the crowd. Lastly, you can come to the wedding prepared with extra copies of the toast in case anyone forgets their own at home.

GUEST SPEAKERS

Inviting in a guest speaker is a great way to add even more value, impact, and/or humor to your toast. However, it is important that this speaker isn't just a crutch to lean on. For example, maybe you are so nervous about getting up and speaking in front of everyone that you let the guest speaker have more microphone time than yourself. Or maybe you are feeling self-conscious about your toast, so you give a guest speaker the freedom to take over the toast and make it more their own. You might also feel like skipping more of the prep work because *it's boring* and decide to just pawn off more of the work onto someone else. First, if you are thinking of taking the lazy route, don't be that person. This isn't about you; it's about the happy couple. So take this honor to heart. Second, if you are feeling nervous about speaking, or worrying about your toast not being good enough, shifting your focus from yourself to the newlyweds can help curb these anxious feelings.

CASE STUDY **Three's a Crowd**

During one wedding toast the two best men brilliantly combined their toasts into one smooth, entertaining speech filled with funny anecdotes, jokes, and celebrations of the significant other (in this case the bride). The crowd was engaged throughout, and anticipated a flawless Big Finish. But as the two men seemed to be wrapping things up, they called a third speaker to the stage. His actual addition to the toast wasn't very long, but by the time he reached the stage, introduced himself, said his lines, and turned things back over to the best men, ten minutes had passed—on top of the ten minutes the first part of the toast had taken. Now twenty minutes long (and still wrapping up), their great toast was quickly losing the audience's interest. It certainly felt like three had made a crowd. If the best men had instead carved out time within their own ten-minute toast for this guest speaker—and limited this guest's time to a maximum of two or three minutes (also factoring in time to get the microphone, introduce himself, and turn things back over to the best men)—it would have worked without a hitch.

If you do choose to have a guest speaker, be sure to keep the following things in mind:

- **Length.** Having more people involved in the speech does not mean the audience wants to listen for twice as long. If you have a guest speaker, keep their participation to two minutes or less.
- **Timing.** When will the guest speaker begin their piece? Will you lead into it by starting a joke they will finish? Will you offer a quick introduction that cues their entrance? Plan this out with them ahead of time, and add any cue notes into your toast. It's also a good idea to give the guest speaker a copy of the whole toast so they can follow along.
- **Location.** Where is this person going to come from? Will they walk over from the head table or guest seating—or maybe burst out of

the cake (with permission from the bride and groom, of course)? Discuss this in advance, and also decide which microphone will be used or how a microphone handoff will occur.

- **Tone.** It's important that your guest speaker's message is either consistent with the tone of your toast (sentimental, funny, etc.), or acts as a purposeful departure from yours—with a smooth transition to get there and another transition at the end to set up your final lines. Otherwise, their addition will feel like an out-of-place tangent in the toast.

- **Impact.** Think about the biggest reason(s) why you feel this guest speaker needs to be a part of your toast. Are they a great friend or sibling of the bride or groom who has something unique to share about them? Do they offer another hilarious perspective of a story you will be telling? Be sure that this person knows their role and can add that value in two minutes or less.

If you parade multiple people up to the microphone like witnesses at a trial, or your combined speech feels like an ultramarathon compared to the other toasts, expect the audience to be silently praying for a microphone malfunction. Make your impact—but don't burn retinas and numb ear drums with a half hour of guest speakers.

CHAPTER SUMMARY

Group or guest speakers can add more perspective, laughs, and happy tears to a wedding toast—if things are done well. If you are part of a group toast, or are considering adding a guest speaker to your toast, here are the main takeaways from this chapter to keep in mind:

- Communication is key! It should happen well before the wedding day, and preferably more than once.
- Some people prefer to work alone and then share notes, while others like a collaborative process. Determine your preferred approach with the other speaker(s) and stick to it.
- Iron out the on-site logistics. From the timing, to verbal and/or nonverbal cues, to the entrance location for the additional speaker(s), the more details you can establish ahead of time, the smoother your toast will be on the big day.

CHAPTER 10

Conclusion: Your Dynamite Toast Checklist

You've made it through the "dos and don'ts," the five critical cogs, tag-team toasts, and everything in between. Now it's go time! You are ready to collect all of your thoughts and notes, write the first draft of your toast, make revisions, and finally raise a glass to the happy couple.

In this conclusion, you'll find your very own comprehensive checklist for brainstorming, drafting, editing, and delivering your wedding toast. You will also discover a simplified version at the end that is perfect for copying and carrying around with you for quick reference. So pick up that pen or pencil and get ready to bring down the house (or, in this case, the reception hall)!

THE CHECKLIST

You may still be a bit nervous about your toast—and that's perfectly normal—but trust that by committing to the following checklist, you will deliver an awesome speech that honors your loved one and their partner, delights the crowd, and lives on beyond just that special day (for good reasons!). All it takes is a few hours of your time, and the tools and new insights you've gained from the previous chapters of this book. You can check off the tasks at home, at a local coffee shop, at a favorite park, or anywhere you feel comfortable and creative. A more condensed, fill-in-the-blank version of the checklist is also available at the end of this chapter.

21 DAYS to WEDDING

■ Spend thirty minutes reflecting and jotting down notes about the couple. Use the Wedding Toast Workouts and questions in Part 2 for guidance.

18 DAYS to WEDDING

■ Spend thirty minutes arranging your notes in the order you will use them in your toast. Refer to Part 2 for assistance in determining the order.

14 DAYS to WEDDING

■ Write a rough draft of your toast and let it sit untouched for at least twenty-four hours.

13 DAYS to WEDDING

- If you are comfortable doing so, share your draft with a close friend or family member.
- Ask that this person give you at least three pieces of constructive feedback about your draft. One of the three comments *must* be a critique or recommendation—this can't just be a rubber stamp of approval.

7 DAYS to WEDDING

- Closely read through your draft (preferably a printed copy).
- Ask yourself whether there are words, phrases, or sentences that don't add any humor, impact, or value to the speech. If so, cut them.
- Ask yourself whether there is anything missing. Do you need one more story, or perhaps something inspiring? If so, make those additions.
- Think objectively about what your reaction would be if someone else gave this toast. Does something just not sit right when you look at it from someone else's perspective? Make any necessary adjustments for the desired reaction.

4 DAYS to WEDDING

- Read the toast out loud to yourself. There may be things that looked good on paper but don't sound right when said out loud.
- Make any necessary revisions following your read-through.

2 DAYS to WEDDING

- Reflect for a few minutes on the entire process of writing the toast. Is there anything that has popped into your head recently that you feel needs to be added?
- Anticipate the reactions of the crowd. Where will you want to pause for laughter, raise your voice, etc.? It can also be helpful to write "(Pause)" into the speech as a reminder to yourself to allow for certain reactions. This will help you avoid rushing through what should be a memorable moment.
- Ensure that you have at least two copies of your toast. It's recommended that you print both of these and put them in pockets of different pieces of clothing you'll be wearing the day of the wedding. You can also email a copy to yourself so you *know* the dog won't make it disappear. And if you decide to read your toast from a digital device, be sure it has plenty of juice by fully charging it the day (or even hour!) of.

WEDDING DAY

- Stand tall, take a deep breath, and give your toast!

MY PERSONAL TOAST CHECKLIST

21 DAYS to WEDDING

DATE _____ COMPLETE (YES/NO) ____

- ■ Spend thirty minutes in reflection about the couple.
- ■ Take notes and record memories that pop up during my reflection.

18 DAYS to WEDDING

DATE _____ COMPLETE (YES/NO) ____

- ■ Spend thirty minutes arranging stories and notes in the order they will be shared.

14 DAYS to WEDDING

DATE _____ COMPLETE (YES/NO) ____

- ■ Write a first rough draft of my toast.

13 DAYS to WEDDING

DATE _____ COMPLETE (YES/NO) ____

- ■ Share draft with someone I trust for honest feedback.

7 DAYS to WEDDING

DATE _____ COMPLETE (YES/NO) ____

- ■ Read through rough draft and make any necessary changes.
- ■ Read the draft out loud from a printed version.

4 DAYS to WEDDING

DATE ▢▢▢▢▢▢▢▢   COMPLETE (YES/NO) ▢▢

- ▪ Do a second read-through out loud.
- ▪ Put myself in the audience's shoes and anticipate their reaction.

2 DAYS to WEDDING

DATE ▢▢▢▢▢▢▢▢   COMPLETE (YES/NO) ▢▢

- ▪ Add in any last-minute ideas or 2:00 a.m. epiphanies.
- ▪ Make sure I have two copies printed (or saved electronically) and ready.

WEDDING DAY

DATE ▢▢▢▢▢▢▢▢   COMPLETE (YES/NO) ▢▢

- ▪ Relax and enjoy the experience!

APPENDIX: WEDDING TOASTS

The following toasts are here to help you in whatever way you need, so you can walk into that wedding ready to deliver a speech you're proud of. You can use them as a jumping off point, examples of the cogs and other toast elements in action, or inspiration if you feel stuck while writing your own toast.

TOAST 1 **DAN AND KATE**

Throughout this book you have read different excerpts from the following speech I made at my brother's wedding. Here it is in its entirety:

> Good evening, everyone. I am Dan's younger brother Pete.
> Many of you I already know; some I have yet to meet.
>
> Dan and Kate, thank you so much for this chance—
> by the way, I call first dance.
>
> I've looked up to Dan ever since I've had sight.
> He was always bigger than me, and he was always right.
>
> Being the oldest of four boys couldn't have been an easy thing.
> But in a house full of hyenas, Dan was the lion king.
>
> I remember building traps in the basement when we were
> all kids,

and how that came to an end when mom tripped on a bunch of well-placed bowling pins (sorry, Mom).

But some of my best memories are days playing running-bases in the yard,
or nights in our bedrooms trading a favorite baseball card.

Or when the four of us would sleep in the same room on Christmas Eve night,
or all the basketball games in the driveway, the video game tournaments, even every fight.

Dan's been an outstanding big brother, I couldn't ask for any more.
Though he did once try to build a campfire in his bedroom and burned a hole in the floor.

pause for laughter

But any time I had questions or problems as a kid, Dan was there to help me through it.
And when I took all the blame for breaking our neighbor's window, *louder* hey, I was glad to do it!

Dan's been and will be a lifelong brother, mentor, and friend to Mark, John, and me, and that will never end.

When he moved from Ohio to Richmond, we were all sad to see him leave.

But he had opportunities to chase, and success to achieve.

Of course, his move to Virginia has led him to Kate.
whether by chance, luck, a love of the eighties, or fate.

And for the entire time I've seen the two of them together,
bright green has been their grass, sunny has been their
weather.

I'm proud of Dan, and really happy to officially welcome
Kate to our family.
You know, it's kind of funny:
Dan's nickname growing up was "the Bear," and this bear
has found his honey.

TOAST 2 **BRIAN AND CARLI**

I wrote this toast for the wedding of my future best man (he absolutely nailed his toast!), Brian, and his bride, Carli. It was good practice for all of the five critical cogs, and a really fun walk down memory lane. Because all of the inside jokes and personal memories about the past are very short and lending to a bigger theme (the repeated question of what to include in my toast), having more of them works better here than it would if each memory were drawn out, or if there were nothing to tie them together at both ends of the toast.

Good evening, ladies and gentlemen. My name is Pete and I've been a friend of Brian's for more than twenty years.

As I was preparing this toast, one question consistently rang in my mind: How do I summarize a friendship that has lasted since we were in kindergarten? Believe it or not, Brian was under six feet tall then—

pause for laughter

But really, how can I possibly speak to all of our experiences in just a few minutes, without it turning into one big inside joke?

I thought, do I talk about how, while he may not have known it, Brian was always a trendsetter that I tried to imitate?

That in fourth grade, when we were finally allowed to wear long ties to school, I wanted in a bad way to buy a Beatles tie because Brian had one.

I didn't know who the Beatles *were*, but I'll be damned if I didn't rent a bunch of their cassette tapes from the library to find out, so I could pretend to be a big fan and wear the tie to school.

pause for laughter

Do I touch on our grade-school recess activities, like our observations of the "Rated R Playground" and vision for a "Hot Teens Nightclub"?

No, I think I'll leave those alone.

But I *have* to mention our unparalleled success as fourth- to eighth-grade basketball players, right?

Four CYO championships in five years, with two undefeated seasons.

…What's that, Jeff? Oh, I need to "let it go"?

pause for laughter

Okay, I'll move on.

Do I mention the BMX years, when Brian had a Schwinn and I had a Dyno, and we cruised around with his brothers and neighbors looking for jumps and dirt tracks to ride?

It probably needs to be said that, while we all thought we were awesome riders, Brian is the only one who ever entered any sort of competition…in which I believe he came in last place.

Do I talk about how my love for music, especially bands like New Found Glory and Blink-182, was heavily influenced by Brian?

I remember when our teacher, Mr. V., took Brian and me to some of my first concerts ever—to see bands like the Goo Goo Dolls and "Weird Al" Yankovic.

Since then we've gone to shows in Columbus and Grand Rapids—and everywhere in between.

The Grand Rapids weekend…
sighs and looks over to the DJ
How much time do I have?

Okay okay…

So do I talk about how most people began referring to us as "Brian and Pete" within the first year of high school, and asked where the other one was if one of us was alone?

Or how Brian grew from being a relatively shy freshman athlete to the best basketball player in the school by his junior year—and prom king as a senior?

Do I talk about how deciding to go to a different college when Brian and I could have been roommates was one of the toughest decisions I've ever made—and how I probably made eight trips to his campus during my freshman year alone?

Or do I talk about the post-college years, when Brian, several of the guys here, and I spent an unbelievable week in Myrtle Beach in 2009?

Folks, come up to me tonight after I've had about four more of these *point to my drink* for some Myrtle Beach stories.

pause

Do I talk a little about basketball coaching with Brian?

How Coach Brian and I spent one year together with the freshmen team, putting together what some (okay, we) have called the greatest, most magical 9–8 season of all time?

Or do I get into so many more of the experiences we've had, whether surviving the Rapture together, taking weekend trips to Columbus, sharing countless jokes, or *the* chicken parm?

No, I'm actually not going to talk about any of those things…

pause for laughter

Instead, I want to talk about how I was with Brian when he met Carli.

How he mustered up the courage to approach and talk to her.

How after their first date, he told me that he could not believe how well it went—how she changed the game for him, and was different from anyone he had gone out with before.

I also want to talk about how it's been a pleasure to get to know Carli.

You know, when they first were dating, I asked Brian what her last name was and he said "Davidson."

Like, "Carli *Davidson*."

I didn't realize he was joking and thought for several months that her family was really into motorcycles.

pause for laughter

And I want to talk about how right I believe they are for each other.

How proud I am of Brian, how much our friendship has meant to me, and how we've got a lot of years ahead of us to soak up the good sun, listen to and make music, watch sports, and make ourselves laugh.

Someday, I'll be taller than him…

But for today, I'll embrace the optics of standing next to him, and keep it "short."

Congratulations to Brian and Carli, and let's all raise a glass to the happy couple.

TOAST 3 **EMILY AND ALEX**

This toast was given by a bridesmaid and close friend (Alice) of the bride (Emily). Alice did a great job of blending fond memories of the bride with funny and touching remarks about the groom. It is a perfect example of short and sweet.

Hi everyone, my name is Alice.

I've known Emily for almost nine years, since we started meeting as part of a book club and realized we'd actually been sitting next to each other in class for months.

We quickly bonded over our love of books and unnecessarily large projects, like donating hundreds of those books to the local library or hand-painting event T-shirts just because "it seemed like a good idea at the time!"

Eventually, Em and I became real friends, beyond the safe little bubble of our school, and I was lucky enough to meet Alex and see what a true bond they have together.

And now Alex comes along for those ridiculous projects, wondering, I'm sure, just what he's gotten himself into.

But whether it's wearing full-coverage face paint for Halloween three years in a row to suit our theme or patiently answering every single dumb question I ask about baseball at a Red Sox game, Alex has never once complained and, I think, is even starting to enjoy himself.

Now, in Kevin's speech he gave you each advice for a successful marriage.

I've never been married, so, unfortunately, I don't have any advice for you today.

Instead, since our friendship originally started because of our mutual love of books and especially fairytales, I thought it fitting that I leave you with three wishes:

For Alex: You have an incredible ability to see the light side of every situation and a dry, witty sense of humor that always has everyone laughing in spite of themselves.

For you, my wish is that you never lose your ability to laugh and that you always remember to share that joy with others.

For Emily: You are one of the kindest people I have ever met, and you're always willing to give everything you have to help others.

For you, my wish is that your generosity is never taken for granted and that you will always receive that same kindness from others.

And last, my wish for you both is simple: May you always find happiness, love, and family wherever you go.

I love you both so much and am so happy to be here celebrating with you today.

I cannot wait to see where this next journey takes you, and I truly believe that the future is brighter for having the two of you in it, together.

Congratulations to Emily and Alex!

TOAST 4 **LIZ AND MIKE**

This toast was given by a friend (Mary) of both the bride (Liz) and groom (Mike). Mary struck the perfect balance between humor and sentimentality in this toast; you can use it as a guide to including the best of both worlds in your own toast.

Good evening.

Thanks Mr. and Mrs. H. for this wonderful party, and for all the fun and generosity leading up to this day—including those drinks at Johnny Mango.

I'm happy to have the opportunity to share a bit about my friends, Liz and Mike.

Liz and I have been friends since our days in high school. I didn't have a huge social circle at school, and felt so cool and lucky to be friends with Liz. And I still feel that way nearly fifteen years later. Mike, I know you feel cool and lucky too.

pause for laughter

A few years after college we both moved back to Cleveland from Chicago and New York around the same time, and ended up living just a walk away from each other's places—which was pretty amazing.

Liz and I had the pleasure of meeting Mike on the same evening a couple of years later. Soon after, Mike divulged that he had seen us around the city for months and always thought Liz was beautiful. I was like, "Um, what about me, dude?"

pause for laughter

But it was clear from the start that Mike only had eyes for Liz, and I honestly wouldn't want it any other way.

They got along easily, shared a sense of humor and values, and things felt different in the best way.

It was also clear that they were going to have some challenges to work through: Liz's favorite food is fries, but Mike is allergic to potatoes; Mike's favorite food is ice cream, but Liz is lactose intolerant…

pause for laughter

Thankfully, things have a way of working out, and we are all gathered tonight to celebrate their love and marriage.

One of the first signs that Mike was going to be around for a while was when Liz casually mentioned that he and her dad were swapping historical novels—plus I think Liz attended more sporting events in the first few months of dating Mike than she had in her entire life.

pause for laughter

Liz, I know you asked your dad not to brag, but you didn't tell me that I couldn't. And with that being said, I'd like to share some of my favorite qualities of Liz and Mike.

Liz: humble, generous, creative, clever, and definitely one of the funniest people I know.

Liz has been known to have certain catch phrases over the years.

For the better part of '06–'07 it was "rowdy." It didn't matter what you said. "Hey Liz, I won't be at lunch. I have to cram for a test." Her response: "That's rowdy."

A more recent is "fire flame track," when referring to a song that she particularly enjoys.

I don't know if she picked this one up from Mike, or if Mike picked it up from her.

Liz is also known for her signature silver linings. If you say to her, "Ugh how is it only Wednesday?" She will likely come back with, "Silver lining: It could be Monday."

And this is a habit that I've tried to adopt as well.

Liz has great taste—from her amazing sense of style to our shared enjoyment of the finer things in life—and I often find myself playing copycat.

She also never shows up to a party empty-handed, and never makes it seem like a big deal.

Her plentiful snacks are just one of the many reasons everyone loves being around Liz.

pause

Mike: passionate, enthusiastic, dedicated, and loyal. Mike doesn't just like ice cream; he loves ice cream. I've heard him say on multiple occasions that he would be at his happiest with his mouth open under the East Coast Custard ice cream spout.

pause for laughter

Mike quickly made himself comfortable in our group of friends. It's not unusual for him to be put on speakerphone while Liz and I are chatting so that he can say hello, or for me to receive a text from him asking me to join them while they're out.

Of course, one of my *favorite* qualities of Mike's is how happy he makes Liz.

pause

Liz and Mike are great, loyal friends. They both have deep love and respect for their families and for each other.

Together, with all of these qualities and more, they make a wonderful team.

When deciding on my roast-to-toast ratio, it was easy to go all in on the toast.

Plus, I think we might be in for a little roast with Bob and Chris coming up next.

pause for laughter

Liz and Mike—this is just the beginning of a lifetime of love. Always remember the qualities that brought you to this moment.

Congratulations and cheers to my friends!

TOAST 5 **LEXIE AND DUSTIN**

This toast was written by the close friend and maid of honor (Kelli) to the bride (Lexie) and groom (Dustin). Note how Kelli grabs the attention of the room right from the opening line, and hits all five of the critical cogs as she works her way through a mix of funny stories and more sentimental moments.

Hi. If you don't know me, you're probably at the wrong wedding because Lex and I have been inseparable for the past twenty years.

pause for laughter

But seriously, my name is Kelli and I met Lex when I was about seven years old at Gymnastic World in Fort Myers.

We quickly became close, as the majority of our time was spent together at Gymnastic World.

When I joined the gym, Lexie was the first person to reach out to me and make me feel comfortable.

From that moment to now, her character has not changed one bit: She has always been the sweetest, most selfless person I've ever met.

Gymnastics was our life.

If we weren't practicing, we were coaching, conducting camp, or hitting the gym.

But if we weren't at the gym, we were hanging out at Lexie's house across the street from the gym.

And if you know her family, then you know that their house was always the house to be at.

There are so many good memories there—like the time we went into her sister's closet and tried on all her dresses and makeup, only to spill her Chanel bronzer all over the floor.

She came home as we were trying to clean it up and hide, but unfortunately we were found.

Or the time we were going to the movies and Lex tried to look so cute while walking down the stairs in heels…and fell all the way to the bottom.

Even years after her family moved to a new home, Lexie and I went back to visit the house.

We knocked on the front door and the new owners answered and then proceeded to give us a tour.

Looking back, that could have gone really wrong and could have easily been the next episode of *Law & Order*.

pause for laughter

Growing up, I always looked up to Lexie.

She is truly like a sister to me; everything she did I wanted to do.

For example, I went to a private high school thirty minutes away because *she* went there.

I turned to cheerleading because she loved it (even though it was totally against gymnastics code).

I even became a diver for a week because she wanted to give it a try.

The best, though, was when I was called out of a class in high school to meet Father Beatty outside.

Of course, I immediately thought I was in trouble.

In reality, Lexie had signed me up to do pole vaulting with her.…That lasted about a day.

There's not one thing that I've gone through in my life where Lex wasn't there for me.

If ever I was sad, she was there to whip out the Oreo ice cream and *Sex and the City* marathon.

Her family is an extension of my family. Brian, Billy, Alissa, Lex, John, and Jay have all had an impact on my life one way or another, and tonight this family grew a little bigger as Dustin and his own family have officially joined it.

I first learned about Dustin in sixth grade when Lexie was talking about a "cute boy from school."

I was actually with her when they met at Bell Tower Shops and he reached out to her on IM.

Though they lost touch, they came back together in high school after a school dance and since that night have had nothing but love for one another.

Dustin, I knew you from the start, and I'm so thankful to have shared so many years with you and Lexie.

Your work ethic and dedication to anything you put your mind to shine through in every part of your life.

Thank you for loving our girl unconditionally. You have stepped in at the hardest times and were not only her rock but all of ours as well.

You are as loyal as they come.

The thing I love most about Dustin and Lexie is that they bring out the best in one another.

They have always been there for each other without any complaints, through the good and the bad.

Lexie, you're my best friend and I love you so much.

We have a quote from years ago that couldn't be more fitting: "Together forever, never apart, maybe in distance but never in heart."

Even though we live apart now, whenever I see you, we pick up where we left off and get abs from laughing all the time—so thanks for that.

You make me want to be a better person every day. I know B is with us tonight saying, "You look beautiful baby."

Lexie and Dustin: I wish you both love and happiness.

Cheers to the bride and groom—love you!

INDEX

ABOUT THE AUTHOR

Pete Honsberger has been a serial groomsman, speaker, and wedding toast advisor for most of his adult life. When it comes to wedding toasts, he's seen just about everything. He has a BA and MA from John Carroll University and resides in Cleveland, Ohio, with his wife, Jenna. You can learn even more about weddings (and perhaps about life) at WeddingToasts101.com.